The I Wills According To SAINT JAMES

By Synthia SAINT JAMES

Dedication

My hope is that everyone who purchases this book will be empowered to use it as their OWN personal affirmation workbook, filling in ALL the empty spaces on each page with their thoughts & desires...

ISBN-13: 978-0615584683
ISBN-10: 0615584683

I0077993

1.   I will believe in miracles.

2. I will open my mind to new ideas.

3. I will find all the joys in life.

4. I will be aware of all the beauty and peace that surrounds me.

5.   I will listen to my own inner alarm system.

6. I will let my pressures ebb away with the tide.

7. I will develop quality attitudes.

8. I will give myself permission to be happy.

9. I will do the right thing at the right time.

10. I will open my way to health and prosperity.

11. I will learn from my mistakes.

12. I will let the joy of life flow freely.

13. I will not give up.

14. I will find a calm center.

15. I will make a restful moment my perfect moment.

16. I will cultivate my inner awareness of right and wrong.

17. I will give willingly and cheerfully.

18. I will choose to be well.

19. I will make the most of all circumstances and then let go.

20. I will reach for the stars.

21. I will forgive so that I will be free.

22. I will determine the ultimate outcome of my life.

23. I will accomplish my goals one step at a
     time.

24. I will show initiative.

25. I will look beyond rejection.

26. I will accept the kinship of all creatures.

27. I will focus on fulfillment.

28. I will sit quietly and reflect on the joy of thinking freely.

29. I will triumph over opposing powers.

30. I will hush my feelings and paint the day the way I want it to be.

31. I will project ahead by looking back objectively.

32. I will rediscover my divine connections.

33. I will keep my beautiful memories alive.

34. I will accept and understand that everything must change as in nature.

35. I will take the time to renew and restore.

36. I will listen for the music in the wind.

37. I will set my goals high.

38. I will make peace.

39. I will allow time for healing.

40. I will feed my spirit.

41. I will grow in wisdom.

42. I will absorb the serenity of nature.

43. I will send out love with a silent touch.

44. I will indulge myself in the glories of nature.

45. I will stay in tune with harmony.

46. I will use my words to empower positivity.

47. I will allow my creative ideas to prosper.

48. I will worship the source of life.

49. I will continuously renew my mind and my spirit.

50. I will take care of myself physically, emotionally and spiritually.

51. I will cherish every moment and every season of my life.

52. I will live my life one day at a time.

53. I will speak positively.

54. I will listen to the inner and outer voices that heal.

55. I will keep my spiritual house clean.

56. I will respect the power of words.

57. I will start each day anew.

58. I will allow others to stand on their own two feet.

59. I will respect the wisdom of elders.

60. I will bathe in sunlight.

61. I will live my life with purpose.

62. I will listen only to positive suggestions.

63. I will lift others up with me.

64. I will boost myself up with the words that I choose.

65. I will see the miracle in each morning's light.

66. I will choose my words wisely.

67. I will face down my fears.

68. I will keep silent until the time is right.

69. I will withhold my opinions of others.

70. I will dwell in the "now".

71. I will greet each day with thanksgiving and praise.

72. I will accept what I can't change and change what I can for the good.

73. I will enjoy the present time, the present company.

74. I will listen to the music of the spirit in all its forms.

75. I will enjoy all the miracles of nature.

76. I will think courage and strength and become just that.

77. I will feel freedom first in my heart.

78. I will make good use of all time because time is so precious.

79. I will solidify my foundations.

80. I will hold the past, present and future dear.

81. I will allow my mind to use the gift of vision.

82. I will protect myself from intrusion.

83. **I will love myself first.**

84. I will take the time to be quiet and recharge.

85. I will realize that an end is also a beginning.

86. I will learn the friendly art of persuasion.

87. I will give people the chance to reveal themselves.

88. I will turn on the joy when times get rough.

89. I will relish my solitude.

90. I will choose the positive.

91. I will harmonize my pulse with that of the
tranquil earth.

92. **I will stand firm for what I know is right.**

93. I will be swept into the beauty of all creation.

94. I will stand firm in what I know is right.

95. I will steadily plant good seeds that we grow into the beautiful plants of success.

96. I will believe in my limitless abilities.

97. I will live and breathe serenity.

98. I will make a place in my life for love, peace and prosperity.

99. I will look my problems in the eye and
     liquidate them on the spot.

100. I will believe that I am essential and have a definite purpose and responsibility.